YOUR IMMORTAL SPIRIT
From Death to Deathlessness

By Bahram Spitama

Table of Contents

About the Author v
Acknowledgements vi
Introduction vii
    Parallel Reality vii
Glossary xii
Chapter 1: The Concept of Time 1
    A Brief History of Measuring Time 2
    Definition of Time 3
    The Linear Time 7
    The Cyclical Time 11
    Eternity 14
Chapter 2: Zarathustra's Concept of Time 18
    The Visible and Invisible World 20
    1. External World (horizontal, linear, visible) 21
    2. Internal World (invisible, vertical,

our state of being) 22
Linear Time 28
Cyclical Time 30
Eternity: The Timelessness 34
Conclusion..**38**

About the Author

BAHRAM MOTERASSED (Spitama)[1] has been a psychotherapist for thirty years, incorporating Eastern spirituality into his practice. He has a BA in psychology and a master's degree in marriage and family therapy. He has studied and practiced Sufism, Buddhism, Yoga, Mazdaism, Christianity, Kabbalah, and sweat lodges. He has also practiced and taught meditation courses for more than thirty years. He is the author of Born to Fly, You Are Beyond Who You Are, Good Thoughts, Good Words, Good Deeds: Thus Spake Zarathustra, Your Immortal Spirit, and From Destiny to Choice.

www.zarathustra.ca

---

1 Spitama is chosen here because of the author's immense love and respect for the wisdom of Zarathustra Spitama.

Acknowledgements

I want to dedicate this book to the Indigenous people of Canada for their spirits of generosity, kindness, and hospitality. Although I have attended therapy and engaged in many other healing practices, my interest in Indigenous sweat lodges persisted for almost ten years. I would also like to dedicate this book to my family in Canada and Iran for their influence. I am thankful for my Persian culture, which has taught me the wisdom of the East. I am indebted to the West, Western culture, and its people, who have hosted me kindly and lovingly over the past forty years. Together, these two cultures have helped me see and understand life from a different point of view. They are not contradicting each other. Instead, they are complementary to one another. I am so grateful to be exposed to both.

Introduction

Parallel Reality

A healer needs healing more than anyone else. I am grateful to have participated in many sweat lodges with various elders among the Indigenous people of Canada for ten years and to have experienced a vision quest from their tradition. Being in these lodges was a spiritual experience and profoundly healing. It feels like returning to the mother's womb. The lodge is hot, moist, and small. The drumbeats resemble a mother's heartbeat. You can hear other people's voices in the darkness, much like a child hears voices from outside the womb. Perhaps it is true that we need to become a child again and start anew, returning to where we were all once pure and innocent.

People enter the lodge by crawling in, recognizing the need to humble themselves in this sacred space. Men and women sit on opposite sides, balancing masculine and feminine energies. The lodge welcomes everyone, regardless of differences in religion, skin colour, gender, social class, or age. Once inside, as chanting, drumming, praying, and singing commence, time seems to dissolve, and individuals enter a trance-like, timeless state. The lodge encourages leaving worldly identities outside and embracing the transformative experience within. I am very grateful for my timeless experiences in the past ten years of practicing with different elders in sweat lodges and my vision quest.

I heard about an Indigenous tradition called a vision quest. In this tradition, an elder puts a person in the middle of a field alone for four days and nights. During this time, the person fasts, meaning they don't eat or drink. In some schools of psychotherapy (Jungian), the therapist may use a similar technique with the clients to help them explore their unconsciousness and for them to connect with their "shadow sides."

Depending on our circumstances, we can be damaged, hurt, corrupted, or wicked in our lives. Our experiences and environment can shape us into something negative or dark. Imagine a potato left to grow in a cramped, dark place—the roots turn twisted. That's like the negative parts of us. They're not really who we are; they're more like unwanted energies, such as depression, anger, or greed, that we pick up along the way. Just like a car gets muddy, our souls can pick up this negative "dirt."

At some point, we have to deal with these negatives and get rid of our negativity deep inside us. We need to become like snakes shedding old skin, letting go of wicket feelings to a healthier ones. We're choosing to be innocent again, like getting new skin and new traits. It is to become a child and to be born again.

In life, we either run from something or toward something. When a wild animal chases us, we flee from danger, even if we're unsure of our destination. On the other hand, when we love something or have a desired goal, we move toward it. Often, what we run from the most is ourselves. We use distractions to avoid facing who we truly are. There is a stranger within each of us, a "me" that we have not taken the time to meet. We are more acquainted with the people and things outside of us than with this stranger residing within.

However, there comes a point when we can no longer run away. We need to cleanse the garden of our being from the weeds of who we are not to nourish the flowers of our authentic selves. To "know thyself" does not happen automatically or naturally. Just as we put effort into getting to know others or acquiring a profession, we also need to put effort and willingness into understanding who we really are and who we are not. There comes a point when we decide to face ourselves.

I found help from an Indigenous elder who guided me through facing myself in a vision quest in Manitoba, Canada, in a place sacred to their tradition. There was a small hill near where I did my vision quest. Many times, I felt like someone was standing there, watching me. It was strange, especially with all my profound experiences and visions, to sense an invisible energy observing me from the hill. Even though no one was there, I couldn't shake the feeling of being watched. A year later, I returned to the same spot. Standing on the hill, I looked down at where I sat during my vision quest. That is when I realized the person watching me was no one else but me. I could see myself sitting there and looking up, wondering who was watching me from the hill. It made me ponder if there is something like a parallel reality. Can we experience different times all at once, I wondered?

The idea of parallel reality suggests many realities happening simultaneously, with different events, people, and outcomes. Each event may come from its own reality, making for a complex experience. If parallel realities are real, it means different timelines exist together. Have you ever felt déjà vu? It is when you feel like you have experienced something before, even if it is the first time it is happening. It is like re-experiencing an event again.

When we consider time, we often view it through a linear lens. It is perceived as the duration of events extending from the past to the present and into the future. Yesterday is gone, and it cannot be revisited. We exist in the present, moving toward the unknown future. The future remains uncertain since it has not occurred yet. Time is like a flowing river. Its current carries events forward, much like water flowing downstream. Just as one cannot hold the water from a river in their hand, similarly, no one can grasp time, currency, or the continuous flow of existence. Living simultaneously in the past, present, and future is impossible. Time means an event that has a beginning and an end.

However, the linear conception of time is not universally shared across cultures. In many historical contexts, time has been viewed as circular and repetitive. Ancient Egyptians, Persians, and Babylonians, similar to Hindus, held a cyclical view of time. This perspective is reflected in the observable patterns of the universe: the Earth rotating around itself and the sun, the repetition of day and night, and the cyclical changes of seasons. Our calendars are designed based on the Earth's rotation around the sun or the lunar cycle, reflecting our connection to celestial movements. Without these celestial movements, our understanding of days and nights and the changing of seasons would not exist.

If time were linear, anticipating crucial agricultural practices, such as knowing when to sow seeds and expecting harvest times, would be challenging. It is intriguing that our clocks operate circularly despite our linear conceptualization of time, with the hands moving in a twenty-four-hour cycle. Have you ever seen a clock reach twenty-five? Clocks function like a merry-go-round, repeating the same cycle of twenty-four hours repeatedly. We call this cyclical movement on a clock 'time,' yet we believe in its linearity.

How about the concept of eternity - timelessness? Eternity has no beginning in it nor any end; it is timeless. Eternity exists beyond the constraints of time. In this book, we will explore the concept of time from the perspective of Zarathustra and ancient Persian culture. Zarathustra lived approximately five thousand years ago in Persia (modern-day Iran)[2]. He perceived human existence in three-dimensional time frames. Our spirits reside in eternal life, but our earthly existence occurs within a temporal duration known as 'time.' In this book, the three different time dimensions from Zarathustra's perspective will be explored.

---

2 The name officially changed from Persia to Iran in 1935.

Glossary

Ahriman	Wicked thought/spirit/energy/anger, *Angra Mainyu* in the *Gathas*, Satan in English
Ahura Mazda	The Sublime Wisdom, the essence, the Supreme Consciousness, God in English both masculine and feminine *Ahura*: masculine, consciousness, light *Mazda*: feminine, wisdom, life
Amesha Spenta	Immortal Bounteous, seven attributes of Ahura Mazda
Angra Mainyu	The spirit of ignorance, unconsciousness, wickedness, anger in English, *Ahriman*, Satan in English
Asha/Artha	Harmony, balance, *Artha*, art in English, harmony
Frashokereti	"Making wonderful/excellent." It is a notion of a final restoration of the universe to its original perfect creation

Fravashi	Authentic self, true self/spirit, our essence, "I," angel, guardian angel in English, "Holy Souls"
Gathas	Songs, the Sublime Songs of Zarathustra composed by himself about five thousand years ago, the only surviving Indo-European language
Mainyu	Mind in English, spirit, energy, way of thinking
Soashyant	Guide, Savior, Messiah in Zarathustra's concept
Spenta	Sacred, holy, progressive
Spenta Mainyu	Sacred wisdom, good mind, progressive mentality, Holy Spirit in English
Spitama	Zarathustra, also known as meaning "pure"
Zarathustra	Zarathustra was an enlightened person who lived about five thousand years ago in Persia (Iran), the founder of the Zoroastrian religion and Mazdaism (seeker of wisdom)

CHAPTER 1

The Concept of Time

Time is an essential factor in the world. Without time, we wouldn't know when it is morning or midnight, what day or month it is, or when birthdays and anniversaries are. We depend on time for all these things. Time is powerful because no one can control it. We can buy many things like cars, houses, clothes, and relationships, but we can't buy time.

The concept of time is very significant in everyone's life since no one can stop it or buy it. It doesn't matter how wealthy someone is when the moment of death comes; even the richest person can't buy more time. We all have a limited amount of it. So it is important to use it wisely. In everyday language, we often use statements to show how important time is. For instance, when we are really into something or enjoying time with loved ones, we might say, "Time flies fast." Of course, time doesn't actually fly, but we mean that we were so absorbed in the moment that we didn't notice it passing quickly.

Another common expression is "Time is money," emphasizing that we shouldn't waste our lives because time is precious. We also use phrases like "Beat the time," "Only time will tell," "Run out of time," or "Too much time on my hands" in both formal and informal conversations. These expressions help us to know where we stand about time and how it influences our experiences. As we have a relationship with someone, we also have connections with time. Time is significant because of each person's limitations on Earth. Once time passes, we can't get it back.

A Brief History of Measuring Time

Time has been an important aspect of human lives since the beginning of our evolution. Our ancestors kept track of time in unique ways by observing nature, such as seasonal changes in the environment, temperature variations, changes in trees and plants, or the migration of birds and animals. These observations helped them understand and recognize the seasons. Our ancestors relied on the movement of the sun and lunar cycles to measure time. They began to recognize that the length of the day changes at various times.

As they observed the sun moving across the sky, they noticed changes in the direction and length of shadows. They invented various devices, such as a simple sundial, to measure the position of the sun's shadow more precisely and determine the time of day. Additionally, ancient Egyptians and Persians developed a **water clock** as a timekeeping device, measuring time-based on the water flow from one container to another. **Candle clocks** were used in ancient cultures. The candle had numbers marked evenly along its length. As the wax burned, it showed a specific period, helping people measure time.

The first **sand clock** was invented in about the 8th century CE. It had two glass bulbs, shaped like cones, connected by a narrow neck. The size and width of the glass determined how much time it could measure. The **sound of bells** at the churches became a significant measurement of the time. In the past, many people used the sound of bells in churches or clock towers to know the time of day. It was until the mid-16th century that the first **pendulum clock** was invented. This clock used the swinging motion of the pendulum to keep track of time.

Now, we have reached a point where we cannot function without a clock, and there is a growing expectation to be punctual and function right on time. Clocks are everywhere—whether we glance at our wristwatches, check the time on our mobile phones, or look at the clock on the microwave, fridge, car, television, computer, in bars, airports, restaurants, bedrooms, or living rooms. Clocks surround us and cannot escape the necessity of functioning around the clock. However, what does time mean? Let's explore its definition from the Western point of view and the Persian, which represents a more Eastern perspective.

Definition of Time

As pointed out, time is often viewed as linear in Western culture, measured by precise standards such as seconds, minutes, hours, and days. However, in Persian culture, time (zaman) is seen as more cyclical and is often connected with nature and the cosmos.

According to the Merriam-Webster Dictionary,[3] time means *duration*. It is *a nonspatial continuum measured in terms of events succeeding one another from past through present to future. It is*

---

3 Time: Merriam-Webster Dictionary
https://www.merriam-webster.com/dictionary/time

an occasion: the point or period when something occurs. It is also a schedule: to arrange or set the time, to regulate (a watch) to keep the correct time.

In Persian culture, zaman (time) means *period, season, and age*.[4] However, it is *not a broad time period*. It is *not the precise time on a clock*. Zaman (time) also stands for death and endings. Time refers to an event or period that starts and finishes. Anything that begins also has an end, just like birth leads to death. However, there are two concepts of time in the ancient Persian Zoroastrian religion. Time was referred to as two-dimensional. In one dimension, time is finite and lasts from birth to death. There is also another time that is boundless and eternal.

In the Gathas (his sublime songs), Zarathustra talks about three kinds of time: linear, cyclical, and eternal. These three dimensions of time coexist simultaneously. Linearly, time is horizontal, moving from the past to the present and into the unknown future. However, eternity is vertical, extending from Supreme Wisdom (Mazda) to Supreme Consciousness (Ahura). It is Ahura Mazda.

---

4 Zaman (زمان). Wiktionary Dictionary
https://en.wiktionary.org/wiki/%D8%B2%D9%85%D8%A7%D9%86#:~:text=%D8%B2%D9%85%D8%A7%D9%86%20(Rumi%20spelling%20zaman%E2%80%8E,period%20of%20time%20in%20history)

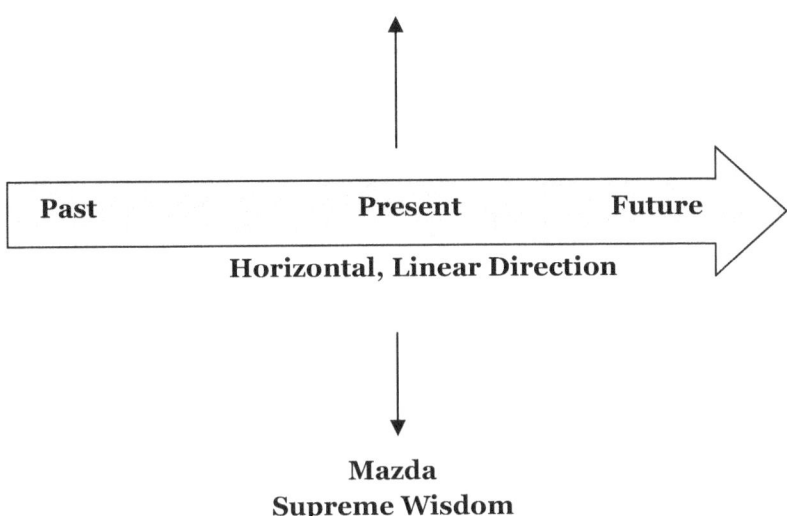

Figure #1: The Linear and The Vertical Time

On linear time and direction, a person is born, grows into adolescence, marries, has children, becomes old, and eventually dies. They go to school, build a career, accumulate wealth, and achieve social status, leaving it all behind upon death.

However, in the vertical dimension, growth refers to the development of consciousness and wisdom. This gain is not material or external but an inner growth. Yeshua (Jesus in Greek) did not possess a university degree, wealth, or material possessions in a linear sense. Instead, he had wisdom. His growth was not marked by external accomplishments but by the wealth of his consciousness and wisdom. On the vertical time dimension, there is always an element of wisdom that remains unknown to us. Wisdom (Mazda) is eternal; it cannot be fully gained or entirely possessed. It is like the horizon: no matter how far we try to reach it, it continually moves further away. One can never fully grasp the horizon. Wisdom is like an ocean with no bottom; the deeper one goes, the more there is to discover and realize. This is why the esoteric school of Zarathustra is known as Mazda-Yasna, meaning the followers of wisdom. They are like divers continuously plunging into the depths of the ocean of existence, seeking pearls of wisdom.

There are two layers of unconsciousness. One is psychological, where painful memories are suppressed and repressed in our psyche. This is a way for individuals to deal with traumatic events and unpleasant circumstances. For instance, someone who was abused as a child might repress the memory as a coping mechanism, detaching themselves from the painful experience. The memory stays in the unconsciousness, and through psychotherapy, clients are encouraged in a safe environment to access these unconscious memories, which have been blocking them from functioning adequately in life.

There is another layer of unconsciousness that is entirely unknown to us. It is not repressed; rather, we are simply unaware of its existence. For example, there was a time when people did not know that the Earth was not flat. We did not know the law of gravity until Newton discovered it and brought it into our consciousness. In vertical time, Mazda or wisdom lies below, as there will always be an element of it that remains unknown to us. It is like a well from which water continually emerges from the source to the surface.

Consciousness (Ahura), on the other hand, is above, like the sun, because it illuminates upon wisdom (Mazda), allowing it to be discovered and known in existence. Life is always evolving, moving from the unknown to the known. Zarathustra refers to this force that drives the universe toward continuous growth as Vahuman, or progressive mentality. Ahura Mazda (The Supreme Being) embodies both Supreme Consciousness and Wisdom. Consciousness is the Seer, and Wisdom is the Seen. Both are eternal, with neither a beginning nor an end. Ahura Mazda is an ocean with no shores.

The Linear Time

Imagine that you came on a train at a station (birth) travelling toward your final station (death). In this metaphor, we all reach a certain point in this train journey and eventually have to leave. It is a journey we must all undertake, depending on our destination. Although we can engage in various activities on the train, such as reading a book, watching a movie, going to a restaurant, looking outside, interacting with others, and taking a nap, we are all confined within this train called time from a linear perspective. We may have choices about what we do and don't do at a certain level, but we don't have the option to go beyond where our ticket is destined to drop us off at our final destination (death). For some, the journey may be short, and for others, a bit longer. Some got on the train before us and left some time ago, while others are waiting to board the train at the upcoming station. However, no one can remain on the train of time forever.

From a linear perspective, everything has a beginning and an end. Whatever comes into existence at some point also has an ending at another point. Eventually, the moon, Earth, and even the sun will vanish and cease to exist. However, do they truly vanish completely? Do we disappear entirely one day without leaving any footprints while we exist? When a deer eats the grass, does the grass die or become a part of the deer? When the tiger eats the deer, does the deer disappear entirely, or does it continue to exist as energy in the tiger's life? Can we genuinely create energy or destroy it? Or does energy transform from one substance to another?

We all know that the heat energy from burning coal in a steam engine can transform into mechanical energy. When we pedal a bicycle, the mechanical energy can transform to power a light bulb on the bicycle. Alternatively, mechanical energy can transform into electricity, allowing us to charge our mobile phones. On a deeper level, is there such a thing as birth and death, or does everything transform from one state to another, similar to a recycling process in a factory?

There is a beautiful story about Buddha's journey toward enlightenment. Originally named Siddhartha, he was a prince in India. Fearing that Siddhartha might renounce the crown to follow a spiritual path, his father over-protected him by shielding him from seeing old, dead, or sick people. Siddhartha always lived in a palace surrounded by young and healthy individuals and never saw dead leaves or an old person. One day, he left the palace with his servant and saw an old man, a dead person, and a sick individual. Questioning his servant about his mortality, Siddhartha learned the truth about aging and death. That night, he left the palace, determined to find a part of himself that would not experience sickness, old age, or death. Eventually, he discovered a timeless aspect of himself.

Similarly, Yeshua (Jesus in Greek)[5] also declared that there is a part within us that transcends our earthly existence and is eternal. The search for it need not extend beyond ourselves, for it resides within each of us.

> *The kingdom of God cometh not with observation: neither shall they say, Lo here! or, lo there! for, behold, the kingdom of God is within you.*

(Luke 17:20-21, KJV)

If a part of us is eternal, is there such a thing as time? Does it really exist that the awakened and conscious human beings invite us to look at our being on a deeper level? Is time a thing in space like we think on Earth, or is it just something humans made up? On Earth, a day is 24 hours, but on Mercury, it is about 1408 hours, and on Jupiter, it is only 10 hours! While a year is twelve months (365 days) on Earth, Mars has twenty-four months in a year. A year on Mars is about twice as long as on Earth. But on Mercury, a year is only 88 days. Interestingly, it takes about 58 Earth days for Mercury to experience a single day, and a year is only about three months (88 days).

Planet	Day Length	Year Length
Earth	24 hours	365 days
Mars	25 hours	687 days
Mercury	1,408 hours	88 days

---

5 The name Yeshua rather than Jesus has been chosen for this book. It needs to be pointed out that Jesus's real name was "Yeshua" in Hebrew and Joshua in English. The name Jesus was given to him by the Greeks years after his crucifixion. However, Jesus's real name was "Yeshua." https://en.wikipedia.org/wiki/Jesus_(name)

The idea of time as we know it on Earth relates to our position about the sun. Our concept of time is specific to our planet and doesn't apply the same way on other planets or in the broader cosmos. Each planet has its unique way of experiencing time-based on its rotation around its axis and the sun. This is a good reminder that time is relative and contextual to where we are in the cosmos.

What we often perceive as time is simply a psychological framework for us to measure duration. Albert Einstein stated that time is relative. When asked to explain this concept in simple terms, he offered an analogy: When sitting next to our beloved for an hour, it feels like a minute, yet during moments of boredom or pain for just a few minutes, it can feel like hours. Whether there is such a thing as time in reality as we understand it, or is time only in our mind?

On a horizontal level, individuals progress externally and materially. The night before, we were sleeping, and today is a new day in which we live our lives, anticipating what tomorrow will bring. The horizontal level is about survival, reproduction, adaptation, wealth and knowledge accumulation, and progress in life. It represents one's external accomplishments from birth to death—a linear line from past to present and into the future.

The linear time is horizontal. It moves from A to B to C to D. It goes in a line. However, eternity is vertical. It is not from A to B and from B to C. It is transforming from A to a higher A to still more to its full potential A. It moves upwards. It is like grape juice transforming into a more mature wine every year. The vertical level is not about quantity; rather, it is about reaching a higher quality. The moment is rare when the inner shift begins when we experience life from a horizontal time into the vertical line.

This transformation opens the door to eternity. In a linear and horizontal life, humans have been searching to find a way to conquer death down the ages. There is no need to search for it when we realize that death is an illusion. It is like a wave that wants to conquer death by disappearing back into the ocean. But does the wave die when it returns into the ocean and becomes one with it again? There is only one secret of immortality and deathlessness. To conquer death is to transcend the mind into the consciousness; to disidentify from our personality (ego) to our spirit and essence (*fravashi*), and to be fully present here and now.

The inner growth, however, can be envisioned on a vertical level. It is the growth of wisdom, love, and consciousness from a lower and animalistic level to a higher and godly level (Ahura Mazda) — a state of timelessness. It is like a tree; the deeper the roots extend into the soil, the higher the tree grows. Have you ever observed a large tree with only a few roots in the ground? On the horizontal level, our existence is bound to our earthly lives on Earth, limited in birth and death, past and future. However, vertically, we connect with a part of ourselves that transcends birth and death, past and future, and temporal existence. It is a part of us that is eternal.

The Cyclical Time

From a circular time perspective, events and experiences repeat endlessly continuously. In this time dimension, we find ourselves entangled in the repetition of natural seasonal, daily, and circular patterns in the universe and our human-made routines, familiarity, and behavioural patterns. Within the cyclical pattern, little change occurs, as days transition into nights, winters into summers, and full moons into new moons. We wake up every day from a specific part of the bed, wash our faces, and brush our teeth, follow specific roads to work or school, return home at a particular time, eat meals in specific manners, watch our favourite shows, and retire to bed at a set time, only to repeat the routine the next day.

We repeatedly engage in the same thought patterns and encounter conflicts with our colleagues, friends, and spouses. Our reactions are often consistent, and we are repeatedly triggered by the same issues. Have you noticed that your issues with your spouses, children, or colleagues tend to be similar? While we may think that human beings are highly unpredictable, observing ourselves and others reveals that we often operate mechanically and robotically for much of our lives. We are very predictable. We become trapped in a circular time fashion, similar to a hamster in a wheel, moving round and round, thinking we are going somewhere. There are two major concepts in cyclical perspectives: **Eternal Recurrence and Reincarnation.**

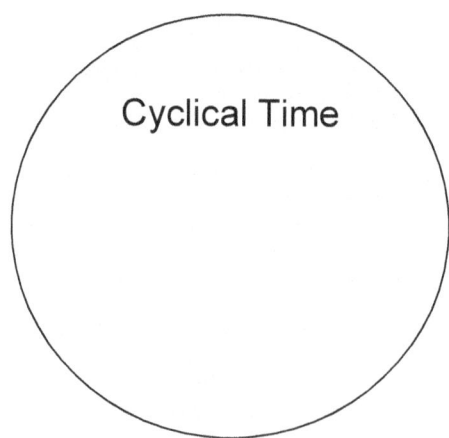

Figure #2: Cyclical Time

Eternal Recurrence: The concept of Eternal Recurrence suggests that time repeats itself in the same way over and over again in an infinite loop of eternity. When we observe the universe, everything returns to its source in nature. Water evaporates from the sea, forms cloud, turns into rain and eventually returns to the sea. A forest may burn in a fire but regenerates in the future. The seasons repeat in a cycle each year. The sunrise transforms into a sunset and renews itself as the sunrise again the next day. Everything follows a cycle of return and movement in nature. Human lives are not separate from this repetitive cycle in the universe. The same pattern also influences our lives. Our past can extend into the present and repeat itself in the future.

There is a saying: *To know our past life, we look at our present circumstances. We observe our current actions to catch a glimpse of our future life.* If the universe continues forever, every event, choice, and experience would happen repeatedly in an endless cycle. However, the idea of recurrence doesn't mean our life experiences are exact copies like a déjà vu. Instead, it suggests that our life events are repetitive, like watching the same movie over and over again. In this never-ending cycle, we can only break free by becoming aware and changing ourselves from within.

Reincarnation is a belief held by many Eastern religions, such as Hinduism and Buddhism. It suggests that the spirit is reborn into different lives, sometimes as a human, animal, or plant. According to this belief, the soul continues to be reborn until it can break free from the cycle of birth, death, and rebirth. Reincarnation is a process for our spirit to purify itself and ultimately reach a state of salvation. Reincarnation is a cyclical concept that believes people are thought to come back to life, encountering the same challenges and errors until they break free from the cycle of life and death. Buddha aimed to free humanity from this repeating pattern, called Samsara.

The evolution of our spirit is like an inner alchemy to escape from the repetition of time. It transforms from our lower self to a higher one (*fravashi*), like a caterpillar turning into a butterfly. Otherwise, we just repeat the same mistakes, sorrows, pain, and suffering.

Eternity

We usually think in terms of time and space here on Earth without much consideration for boundlessness and eternity. However, beyond time, there exists another state called eternity, which is timeless. It is time without end. It is a duration without any beginning or an end. Eternity means there is no beginning and no end. It is like a spiral evolving from the unknown to the unknowable. Eternity is connected to timelessness, whereas infinity is more about endless numbers. We can view eternity like the infinite sequence of numbers from -1, -2, -3, -4... to +1, +2, +3, +4... It goes on without limit.

We can't feel eternity if we are attached to the mind and stuck on our personality. Eternity is felt when the mind is quiet, and not a single thought hides the sun of consciousness, just like clouds on a starry night. It is like trying to see the vast sky and stars on a cloudy night— is it possible? Similarly, we can only sense our eternal essence when we detach from our personality and the mind.

In Buddhism, reaching enlightenment is called the "great death." We must release our perceived identity to find our true essence. Buddha's path to enlightenment is called nirvana, derived from Sanskrit, meaning cessation, extinction, and disappearance. It is a state of freedom where you are set free from your personality and earthly desires, blending into the universe and becoming one. It is about reaching the part of ourselves that is boundless and timeless.

Similarly, Yeshua (Jesus) emphasized the need to be born again as our true selves (spirit) to experience the eternal, as mentioned multiple times during his ministry.

I tell you the truth: no one can see the kingdom of God unless he is born again.[6]

The wind blows wherever it pleases. You hear its sound, but you cannot tell where it comes from or where it is going. So it is with everyone born of the Spirit."[7]

In Sufism, there is a saying: "die before you die." It doesn't mean physical death but encourages us to stop identifying with our bodies and recognize our immortality. It is about annihilating our current self (*fana*) to indeed exist eternally (*baga* - subsistence). It is not hard to observe and experience a different state of trance and timelessness during Sufi practices like chanting, *Zikr* (self-remembrance), and whirling. In Persian literature, many Sufis are referred to as mad or drunken due to their state of annihilation.

One of the greatest Sufi mystics, Halaj, underwent the annihilation of his human experience. In that state, there was nothing left of him except the divine. When he declared, Anā al-Ḥaqq (I

---

6 John 3:3 NIV

7 John 3:8 NIV

am the Truth, I am God) since only God is the Truth, people did not understand his state of being at his time. He wasn't claiming to be God but expressing that nothing else remained in him except God - Haqq.

Like a musician lost in the music or a painter absorbed in the canvas, it is as if they enter a trance — a timeless state. The musician becomes the music, and the painter becomes the painting, merging into each other and uniting as one. In Hinduism, *Moksha* means freedom, freeing ourselves from the illusion of linear and cyclical time (*Maya*) to see who we are in eternity.

Zarathustra calls this awakening to our higher consciousness a state of paradise. When we are not bounded with the linear time frame and we connect ourselves to the Supreme Being (Ahura Mazda). The word paradise is a Persian word from Zarathustra's concept of when existence was in harmony and peace and functioned based on order (Asha). Zarathustra also calls it "House of Song,"[8] "House of Light, or Good." The word paradise (Heaven, Garden of Eden) comes from the ancient Persian term *"pairi-daeza,"* meaning *"enclosed garden."* "The word *paradise* originated from Old Persian *pairidaeza*, which meant "walled enclosure, pleasure park, garden." *Pairidaeza* came into Hebrew, Aramaic, and Greek retaining its original meanings."[9] It is a state of being fully conscious by being aware of our thoughts, words, and actions. It is the state of allying our

---

8 Yasna 50.4

9 Paradise. Encyclopedia.com. 2018.
https://www.encyclopedia.com/philosophy-and-religion/other-religious-beliefs-and-general-terms/religion-general/paradise

consciousness to the Supreme Consciousness and Mind[10] based on good thoughts, good words, and good deeds.

Figure #3: Ahura Mazda

Vahishta Mana - The Sublime Universal Mind

The source of Consciousness

and Wisdom (Goodness)

---
10 Vahishta Mana - The Sublime Universal Mind (Ahura Mazda)

CHAPTER 2

Zarathustra's Concept of Time

There are three frameworks to perceive phenomena around us: 1. Logical, 2. Negation, and 3. Wholeness. Logically and linearly of perceiving life, everything is either/or. Two things cannot coexist at once. You are either in London or Paris; you cannot be in both places simultaneously. Similarly, you cannot be both yourself and someone else at the same time. Elvis Presley is not John Lennon, and vice versa.

In the second approach (negation), whatever we perceive is not definitively true. It is neither this nor that. However we attempt to explain the divine, it is neither this nor that. We struggle to grasp an absolute truth; whatever explanation we provide, the truth is neither this nor that. It doesn't matter how long you may know someone; we do not know precisely how the other person feels and experiences life.

In Hinduism, it is believed that we have forgotten who we truly are. To inquire and "know thyself," one must approach it through negation, a practice called *Neti, Neti,* which means "neither this, nor that." The real self is beyond any description. While we don't know exactly who we are, we do know who we are not. By negating every definition of who we are—our gender, names, education, ethnicity, or career—we reach a point where nothing is left to define us. The part that remains undefinable is who we really are. Buddha used a metaphor of an onion to illustrate this concept. By removing and negating all the layers of an onion, one eventually reaches a point where nothing remains. This cessation into nothingness, he called *Nirvana*.

On the other hand, the third approach is holistic. Everything is interrelated. Everything is both this and that. You can be a father and a son simultaneously. Someone can be a dentist, a father, a son, and a swimmer all at once.

Separation is merely a mind's illusion. The mind tends to categorize, separate, label, and distinguish things from one another. Thanks to the mind, we can recognize our mother from our father, our shoes from our hats. However, are things truly separated from one another? Is your head apart from your feet or your heart apart from your lungs? In reality, you are the head, the feet, the heart, and the lungs.

Similarly, are the colors of a rainbow truly separated from each other, or do they all originate from a singular sunbeam? Are we genuinely separated from one another, with our planet Earth isolated from the rest of the cosmos, or do they all unite? In the broader perspective, we are all interconnected and bound by both this and that.

There was once a mystic whose wisdom was greatly admired by the king. To express his gratitude, the king invited the mystic to his palace and offered him a precious pair of golden scissors as a gift. The mystic looked at the scissors, then returned them to the king and asked for a needle instead. He explained to the king that the function of scissors is to cut and divide, which goes against his approach. As a mystic, he sews and unites like a needle, not bringing division like the scissors.

Zarathustra's approach to life is all-inclusive and holistic. His aim is to unite, not to divide. He views time within linear, cyclical, and eternal dimensions. Our lives unfold in a linear time frame marked by birth and death, past and future, and cyclical patterns involving repetition and natural cycles. Simultaneously, there is an eternal and timeless aspect within each of us.

The Visible and Invisible World

Zarathustra speaks of both a visible and invisible side in each of us.[11] Physically, we live in a tangible world of matter, experiencing space and time. Simultaneously, we have a spiritual aspect in the invisible realm of the soul and spirit, existing in a state of being. Emotionally and mentally, we go through various states, like calm or restless. Our awareness is confined to our current state. Likewise, in the invisible realms of emotion, mind, and spirit, we exist in states, not spaces.

When we use a table, we usually only see its external, visible part. We are often unaware of the many invisible layers hidden from our view. Consider the tree in the forest from which the table originated. What about the woodcutter who felled the tree, the truck and its driver who transported it to the factory, the factory owner and workers who crafted the table, the store where it was bought, or the salesperson who sold it to us? Behind the visible table are numerous invisible factors, and we can't ignore the energy and spirits involved.

---

11 Gathas: Yasna 31.11

Similarly, when we look at a painting, we only see the visible part before us. Yet, what about the painter, their energy, mood, or state of being while creating the artwork that is not immediately visible to us? When we look at water, can we see the H2O in it? We can't see the invisible presence of Hydrogen and Oxygen, but we can't deny their existence in the water.

Have you noticed everywhere you go, there is a different energy behind the place? A rose garden has a different energy than a graveyard. There is a different energy in the airport and the mall than you might feel in a library. Even your own energy and mood can vary day to day or upon certain circumstances. So, it is not just the physical and visible part of something that is important. The energy behind the physical object is also a very crucial factor. Zarathustra calls this energy "spirit," or "mind - Mainyu."

Zarathustra believes that there are two fundamental energies (minds, spirits) in the universe: The progressive, uplifting, conscious energy that he calls *Spenta Mainyu* (the sacred mind/spirit). And there is also another invisible energy that creates stagnation, deception, dullness, and destruction. He calls it *Angra Mainyu* (the wicked mind or Ahriman).[12]

1. External World (horizontal, linear, visible)

We experience the External World through our five senses. We often focus on our external identity, like career, gender, name, body size, appearance, or social status, rather than being aware of our internal world. Our perception of who we are is often

---

12 Gathas: Yasna 30.4

tied to these external factors, and this is the world of space and time. Space and time are part of the external world.

2. Internal World (invisible, vertical, our state of being)

A. Soul — This is about our internal emotions and thoughts, like how we feel and think. It involves our psychological state — whether we're happy, sad, worried, or overthinking. It's about our perception of events and how we judge people.

B. Spirit — This is our essence, our true being, often referred to as "am-ness" or *fravashi*. It's our connection to the spirit world through consciousness, meditation, prayer, visions, or dreams. In the spirit realm where we experience timelessness and eternity.

While there are many theories about human personalities from different schools of psychology, we first need to know what the term personality means. Personality comes from Greek dramas — *persona*. It refers to a theatrical mask worn by performers according to their roles in ancient Greece. In those dramas, each player would have to wear a mask. They used to call the mask a persona, and the character created by that mask was called the personality. They were acting out something they were not. Similar to the mask, our personality means that which we are not. Our true face and self are hidden behind it.

Our persona (personality) is the mask that we wear in order to present ourselves according to our social settings. Just as the Greek actors whose real faces were covered by the mask (persona), our real self is masked by our personality. It is like a cloud blocking the sun. Personality is limited, and it creates an illusion of separation between us and our surroundings. It also gives a false idea of who we really are. Personality is like a fake coin. It looks real, but it does not have any value. Our personality is a counterfeit version of ourselves.

As our identities began to shape, we moved further and further away from our true self (spirit). It is like the ancient Greek actors who may start forgetting their original faces under the masks (persona). They may begin to identify more with the masks and their roles on the stage than with who they truly are. One may play the role of a king on the stage, and he may still act like a king when he leaves the theatre in real life. Indeed, we all become like actors trying to fit into a role on the stage of life and finding an appropriate script to perform our lives accordingly.

In order to come to know our essence and true self (spirit), we need to drop all the clothes of the personality. In Zen, it is called finding our original face. Yeshua said to become a child again. The clothes of personality need to be dropped not only externally, but also internally — in our minds — in how we perceive ourselves. When we are in touch with our essence, there is a sense of unity and wholeness. In essence (spirit), we are all one. In personality (soul), we are many and fractured. If we pour water into different shaped containers, add colours to them, and freeze them, the ice cubes are all different shapes and colours, but they all have the same source — water.

When we realize that the masks — our personality — are just a social identity, we can drop them any time and become naked to our being and our essence. There must be an inner separation within us between our essence (spirit) and personality (soul).

The inner separation helps us see our personality through the eyes of the essence—the inner eyes. By emptying ourselves of the personality, the essence begins to emerge. It is like we have a rose garden, but there are too many weeds that prevent us from seeing the roses. First, we need to distinguish the roses from the weeds. Then, by removing and emptying the garden of the weeds, the roses become evident. Personality is like the weeds surrounding the essence in the garden of our being. Personality is like a dark cloud that blocks the sun. The sun is always there to give us true life, light, and warmth. However, the clouds are obstacles to the sun.

Disassociating oneself from personality (soul) brings authenticity since personality is false, pseudo, fake, and phony. We were not born with it. It was imposed on us after birth from the outside. However, our essence is what we bring into the world from beyond. Essence is not egoistic. In contrast to personality, it does not have a sense of "I"; it is pure "am-ness." It carries the wisdom of existence and contains the seed of our higher being. Knowing our essence means knowing the immortal part of ourselves. The body, mind, emotions, and all our identities die one day (soul), but there is a part within (spirit) that does not have any beginning nor ending.

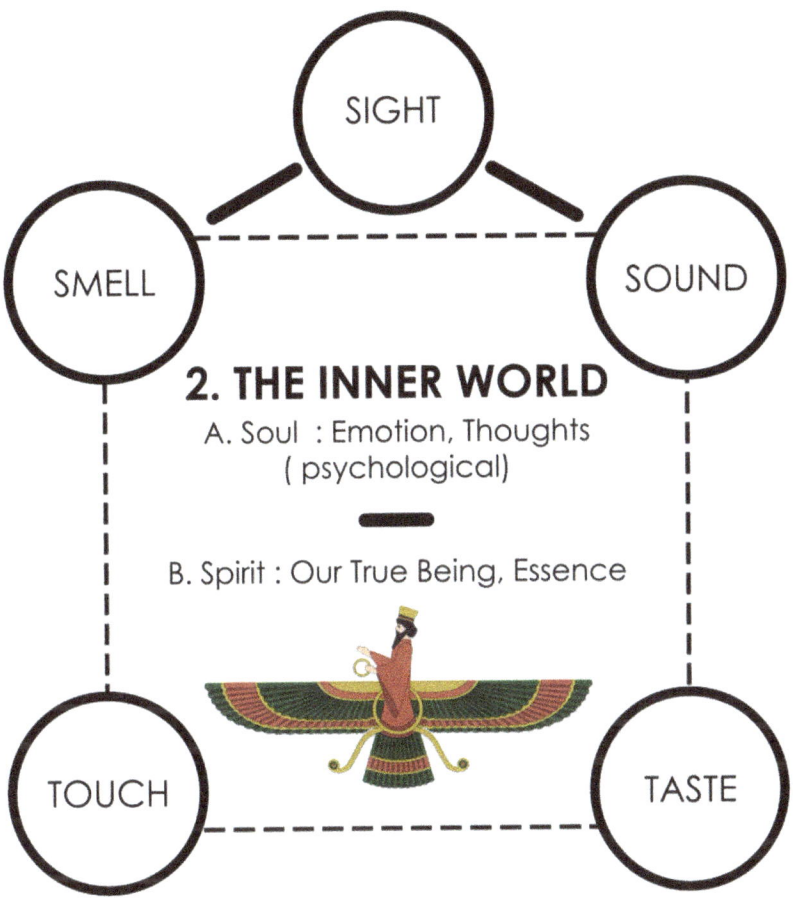

Figure #4: The visible and invisible worlds

We can observe all these three levels simultaneously. We have a body living in a material world. We have psychological existence through our thoughts and emotions that are invisible (soul). And we have a spiritual existence that is eternal and timeless. When we observe ourselves, we can detach ourselves from the body and the soul to be fully aware of our spirit during meditation. When we are entirely conscious, we are connected with our spirit. When we are unconscious and on autopilot, living a mechanical life, we are caught in the mind, emotion, and body in the realm of time (soul).

At the moment of death, our physical body and our spiritual part of ourselves begin separating. Usually, the body, soul, and spirit are so involved with each other that we cannot experience their separation. But at the moment of death or meditation, they begin to be unidentified with each other. Now, their directions will be different; the physical body returns to the physical elements - from dust to dust. And the spiritual body is on its pilgrimage toward the spiritual realm. If we were able to understand that we are neither this body nor our mind or emotion during our life span, but we are something formless and a pure consciousness. Our death would be conscious and have a different experience. Spiritual practices aim to experience the eternal part in ourselves and to transform death into the realization of deathlessness in our core being.

By being connected fully with our spirit, death is no longer death. We are in touch with part of ourselves that will not be destroyed or die. We realize that we are part of life and that life cannot be destroyed! Life is eternal, and death is just a shift from one level of being to another. It is like shifting the energy from flowing rivers into electricity. The river's power doesn't die; instead, it transforms into another form of energy. Death is not against life. It complements life like night and day, hot and cold, or dark and light.

Let's revise our concept that life is short. How about when we start to realize through our spirit that life is not short, but it is eternal. Then, what is all this rush and all the hurrying about?

Don't we miss life when we are in a hurry? Nothing in the universe is rushing to get somewhere since everything in nature comes exactly on time without hurrying. Except humans, the whole existence seems to be aware of the eternity of life. Rivers flow, seasons change, flowers bloom, and trees grow when their time comes without running faster than the natural determination.

There is a story about a king who dreamed of dying at sunset the next day. When he woke up, he felt anxious and worried. His advisors tried to explain the dream, but he wasn't comforted. One advisor suggested he ride far away on the fastest horse before sunset and return afterward. The king liked the idea, and raced away as far as he could from the palace. After a long and fast ride, he found a garden to rest in. As the sun set, when he was resting under a tree, he saw his enemy, who had given up on attacking him and was planning to return to his country. The enemy was amazed that the king had rushed right into danger. He said to the king, "If you were not in such a rush to get here today, perhaps you could be alive tomorrow."

Perhaps, like the king, we rush without knowing where we are headed. Can our body, mind, and being handle this fast pace through 'time'? Maybe we should re-learn the art of being. Doing is tied to time and space — it is linear. Being is linked to our essence, our timeless core existence when we are present here and now.

According to Zarathustra, we live in an evolving and growing universe. Like a candle whose flame is never the same and continuously changing, life keeps evolving, reaching into higher and higher stages. But there is no end anywhere. How can there be an end when there is no beginning in the core of our existence? We, as spirits, exist like a tightrope walker between a beginningless life and an endless life. We exist and always walk in the middle of both sides of these two valleys.

Linear Time

As it was pointed out, anything with a birth has a death. Anything created has an ending and is viewed in the frame of linear time concept. According to Zarathustra, there was no time before creation. There was an eternity. Only the Absolute (Ahura Mazda) existed eternal. However, the linear time began when Ahura Mazda created the twin spirits of *Spenta Mainyu* (the sacred mind/spirit) and *Angra Mainyu* (the wicked mind or Ahriman).[13]

In *Yasna 30.3*, Zarathustra introduces the original concept of linear time in creation. He declares that, **in the beginning**, two primal or twin spirits were created, marking the starting point of linear time. Moving to *Yasna 30.4*, Zarathustra emphasizes that at the end of creation, these twin spirits differ in thoughts, words, and actions until the end of the world. One spirit is progressive and conscious, while the other is destructive and opposes life as long as the world exists.

Despite the varying lifespans of creatures such as mosquitoes (ranging from 10 to 58 days), cats (approximately 14 years), and humans (an average of 70 years), all creations, including the primal spirits, experience birth and death. There will be an end to their existence as well.

In the early days of creation, when the twin spirits came into being linearly, the Supreme Being crafted existence to be perfect.

---

13 Yasna 30.3

Both spirits were neutral in the spirit world. However, as the material world, the third level of existence, was formed, corruption started to influence humans' minds.

The beginning of the creation was the "golden age" as a paradise. According to the Gathas, the world was created perfectly like a paradise. The twin spirits of *Spenta Mainyu* (the Sacred Spirit) and *Angra Mainyu* (the Wicked Spirit) were natural at the beginning of creation. *Yima* (*Jamshid*) was a mythical king who was chosen by Ahura Mazda at the golden age to protect peace and prosperity on Earth. However, he became corrupted by the Wicked Spirit and his followers by eating meat, slaughtering animals and cows, and spreading lies and deception on Earth.[14] He became egoistic by asking people to praise him more than the Divine. As a result, the Wicked Spirit became active and entered the world through human choice for corruption. That was the beginning of the formation of personality: a separate identity from the authentic self (spirit).

Through human minds, the Wicked Spirit will spread wicked deeds throughout the Earth by its followers until a new awakening occurs among humanity to bring truth, order, and harmony (Asha, Artha, art in English) back again. Throughout history, many messengers and saviors (Saoshyant's)[15] will come to guide humanity toward perfection, peace, and harmony again. The Earth will return like a paradise again, and the light will shine over darkness.

---

14 Yasna 32.8-11

15 Zarathustra's term as a savior in the Gathas is "Saoshyant," which translates to "savior" or "benefactor."

Cyclical Time

As pointed out before, everything goes back to its source in nature when we observe the universe. Water evaporates from the sea, forms cloud, turns into rain and eventually returns to the sea. If the universe continues forever, every event, choice, and experience would happen repeatedly in an endless cycle.

There is a term in Zoroastrian tradition known as **Frashokereti.** It means "making wonderful / excellent." It is a notion of a final restoration of the universe to its original perfect creation. The Light will overcome darkness; Truth will win over lies and deception. The world will be reconstructed and governed by wisdom and consciousness again in perfect unity with the Supreme Being (Ahura Mazda).[16] *The world will be restored to its ideal condition.*[17]

According to the *Frashokereti* idea, humanity experiences a dark time in their lives. Ahriman (the Wicked Spirit) will dominate the Earth, spreading lies, deception, corruption, violence, and greed. However, there comes a time that humanity will wake up to its own true nature of "goodness," "wisdom," and "consciousness."

With the guidance of *Saoshyant's* (guides, saviors), humanity will make the Earth like a paradise again. Humanity will regain "the golden age" of the original creation of peace and prosperity on Earth. Zarathustra was a *Saoshyant*,[18] a savior of humanity to guide us toward healthier and more conscious life on Earth. He hoped that this restoration would occur by

---

[16] Yasna 30.8
[17] Yasna 30.9
[18] Yasna 50.11, Yasna 29.6-11

the end of his life.[19] However, he also pointed out that other *Saoshyant's* and saviors would come after him to complete his mission and teachings on Earth.

However, since Zarathustra emphasizes everyone's responsibility for their thoughts, words, and actions, the coming of the Saoshyant (messiah) does not mean that we should wait for them to come and save us from the corruption and chaos in the world. According to his teachings and the concept of Frashokereti, everyone is also responsible for bringing the world back to its original goodness. We all have an active duty towards the world's fate, working to make it a paradise again. Our task is to enhance our wisdom and awareness while safeguarding the Earth, all living creatures, and our existence.

The Persian calendar, historically based on astronomical observations of cyclical shifts in nature aligning with agricultural and seasonal activities. Zoroastrians pray five times a day towards the sun depending on its location from the sunrise to the sunset. There are two major cyclical festivals in Persian calendars: *Nowruz*, and *Yalda*.

Nowruz is celebrated on the first day of spring (March 20 or 21), when nature renews itself after the cold winter. Nowruz means "a new day." It marks the end of an old life and the beginning of a new life for us. It is the victory of life (spring) and light over darkness and lifelessness of winter. It is the Persian New Year, celebrating the arrival of spring and marking the beginning of the year in the Persian calendar.

Another celebration from ancient Persia to date is *Yalda* based on the appearance of the sun *Mithra* (sun) during the winter

---

19 Yasna 48.2, Yasna 34.15, Yasna 46.19

solstice. *Mithra's* birthday was traditionally celebrated in Persia for over 7000 years on Dec 22. *Yalda* means "birth." It was a celebration of both *Mithra's* birth and the Winter Solstice. *Yalda* is still celebrated in Iran and is associated with the birth of Savior, *Mithra*. It symbolically represents the 'victory of light over darkness.' *Yalda* happens around 21 December, the longest night of the year, thus the beginning of the longer days. The Sun (*Mithra*) is born. It marked the return of the sun since days began to get longer.

> *In Zoroastrian tradition the longest and darkest night of the year was a particularly inauspicious day, and the practices of what is now known as "Shab-e Chelleh/Yalda" were originally customs intended to protect people from evil during that long night, at which time the evil forces of Ahriman (evil) were imagined to be at their peak. People were advised to stay awake most of the night, lest misfortune should befall them, and people would then gather in the safety of groups of friends and relatives, share the last remaining fruits from the summer, and find ways to pass the long night together in good company. The next day was then a day of celebration…[20]*

Although the time of creation of the Twin Spirits and their end is linear, the Frashokereti concept holds a cyclical idea from Zarathustra's point of view.

---

20 Wikipedia. Yaldā Night
https://en.wikipedia.org/wiki/Yald%C4%81_Night#In_film

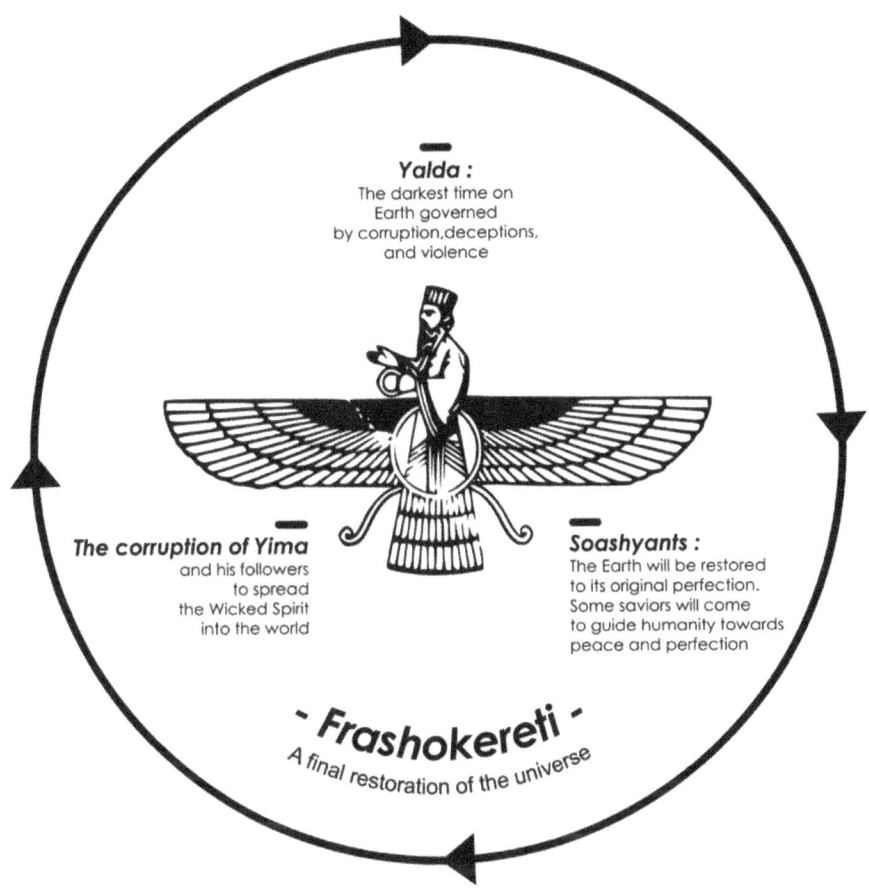

Figure #5: *Frashokereti* - The Cyclical Time in the Gathas

A final restoration of the universe to its origin of
Paradise (perfection)

In the Cyclical idea presented in the Gathas, the creation returns to its original perfect condition. This recurrence of the cosmos to its nature of goodness is the world at the end of linear history. We will once again reexperience paradise on Earth. Our spirits will wake up to its source of wisdom and eternal life in paradise.

Eternity: The Timelessness

As it was mentioned before, we live in two worlds simultaneously — the visible world and the invisible world. The visible world is our external parts, such as our bodies, and what we experience outside of ourselves. In the external world, we are captured in the prison of time from the past to the present and tomorrow. We are all trapped in the linear time frame in our corporeal world.

The symbol of Zoroastrianism, the *fravashi*, stands for the eternal spirit inside us. Ahura Mazda is immortal, with neither a beginning nor an end. When we become aware of our true self, we transcend mortality. Even though the body may disappear, a part of us (*fravashi*) remains undying and immortal.

Figure #6: Symbol of Fravashi

The Holy Soul, true self/spirit, our essence

Fravashi (spirit) is our eternal part of ourselves that will exist in the eternal world even though our physical bodies will end one day. Within us, there exists a part of Ahura Mazda known as *fravashi* — our true essence. It is a spirit that existed before our current life and will endure after death. Our essence, known as *fravashi*, is considered sacred. It predates the universe's creation and can be envisioned as a human-like figure with two wings. In Zoroastrianism, *fravashi* carries significant symbolism, representing our true and real selves and even a connection to the divine self. The central circle around fravashi's trunk symbolizes the immortal nature of the spirit, reflecting eternity without a beginning or end.

We're often unaware of or connected with our true self (*fravashi*). We are born with our essence, but it's like a hidden seed until we nurture and develop it. The path to spiritual life doesn't rely on personality since it mainly operates in society. An apple seed won't grow into an apple tree unless we plant it in the soil, provide water, and care for it. Growing the seed into a tree requires effort and attention. Eventually, when the tree matures, it bears fruit — apples. But this growth process can't happen unless we nurture the seed. Similarly, we must cultivate the seed of *fravashi* in our consciousness. We need to nurture consistently and tend to it through our thoughts, words, and actions to fully develop it into a "Mazda-like" state.

Our true self is like a dimmer switch. It starts from a dark and low point, and as we gradually increase its brightness, our inner world becomes fully illuminated. Through embracing our authentic self, our awareness expands, making us more receptive to Mazda's love and wisdom. Hence, in our spiritual journey, the most crucial task is to be open and receptive to Mazda's presence. Surrendering is essential for spiritual growth.

Zarathustra emphasizes surrendering not to a specific person or belief but to divine love and consciousness.

Zarathustra points out in the Gathas that the followers of truth and wisdom shall attain 'the Abode of Light," "the paradise."[21] They shall be given to them perfection and *immortality*.[22] Zarathustra, as a *Soashyant* (a guide), asks the Supreme Being (Ahura Mazda) how to bring to humans the gift of Perfection and Immorality as was promised by Ahura Mazda.[23] In Yasna 45.7, Zarathustra emphasizes again that the people who follow the Good Mind, Wisdom, Consciousness, and Truth shall be rewarded immortality. It suggests that the spirits of these conscious and wise human beings will experience eternal glory and brilliance in the "House of Light, or Good - paradise."

Based on a few examples from the Gathas and many other verses, Zarathustra believes that there is an immortal part in us that needs to be awakened by the spirits of love (*Armaiti*), consciousness and wisdom, good mind (*Vohuman*), balance and order (*Asha*), perfection, and willpower. Since Ahura Mazda is the Supreme Wisdom and it is Immortal, we can connect with the seed of our own immortality when we are tuned with the above attributions of the Supreme Being within us.

The spirit is like our core, our true self that has been with us even before birth and will continue after we are gone. Our most genuine self is the real "us," "the Godly self." It has a connection to something divine and has the potential to be "Godlike." This part of us holds the potential for a higher level of "goodness"

---

21 Yasna 31.20

22 Yasna 21.21

23 Yasna 44.18

beyond our earthly understanding. It carries the divine's attribution of what it is to be "good." While we may deny everything outside of us, we cannot deny our true existence within.

One day, some friends unexpectedly went to visit another friend. When the host heard knocking at the door and wasn't ready for company, he opened the window and told his friend outside, "Sorry, I'm not home right now. Come another day when I am home." Denying the existence of our essence (*fravashi*) is like the host claiming not to be at home. But who is in the background observing our thoughts, words, and actions? Who is the one that puts us to sleep and wakes us up every morning? Who is the true host, and who are the guests coming and going? Our thoughts, emotions, events, and people may come and go, but there's a part of ourselves that's always present that we cannot deny: our true self, our essence, *fravashi*.

Conclusion

Linear time plays a crucial role in our lives. It shapes our experiences and defines our existence. From the moment we are born to the time we pass away; every event is connected to a particular moment in time. The universe itself is in constant motion, evolving and transforming as time progresses. As individuals, we also change over time. Who we were a decade ago is not who we are today.

Each moment brings new experiences, challenges, and opportunities, shaping us into the people we become. No two moments are exactly alike; each one is unique and holds its unique importance. Life is like a river, flowing continuously forward. Just as we cannot step into the same river twice because the water is constantly moving and changing, we cannot re-experience the same moment in time. Everything around us is in a state of flux, and it is this constant change that defines the journey of life.

Humans have relied heavily on clocks in their daily lives for the past few centuries. To fit into society, we must follow strict schedules, such as starting and finishing work on time. Punctuation is essential for catching flights and buses and attending events like movies or sports. With their red, yellow, and green signals, the precise timing of traffic lights is crucial for preventing chaos and ensuring smooth traffic flow at intersections.

Time can be perceived through two distinct lenses: quality and quantity. Quality of time is about the experiences we have. Depending on what we are doing, time can seem to pass quickly when we are having fun or go slowly when we are bored. Quantity of time, though, is about how long something lasts from start to finish. For instance, a movie might take two hours, while a TV show might only last one hour. This side of time is about how much time we spend on an event.

In the Western culture, we are time obsessed. The reason behind it is that we perceive our life on earth only once, from birth to death, and that is it. If we believe in only one life on earth, making the most of our twenty-four hours makes sense. We have only one birth and one death. They are both absolute. There is a pressure that a single moment cannot be lost. If it is lost, it cannot be regained. Many individuals stay busy, juggling various tasks, but often forget to "be" in the present moment. It is like a customer expecting good service for the money they have paid; similarly, we all desire the best returns from our investments in our daily and lifetime experiences on Earth. The constant pressure of time affects us mentally, emotionally, and spiritually in different ways.

In certain Eastern beliefs that support the concept of reincarnation, there exists a different perspective on time compared to Western cultures. The notion of time isn't as pressing since individuals are believed to experience a continuous cycle of birth and rebirth. This cycle reduces the need to rush through life, as there is an understanding that lost experiences and opportunities will recur again and again in future lives. In these perspectives, the linear progression of birth and death isn't seen as absolute.

Instead, the cosmos is viewed as operating circularly, where birth leads to death and death leads to rebirth. This cyclical nature suggests that nothing is truly lost, as all experiences and relationships have the potential to be revisited in the next birth. This perspective mirrors nature, where everything moves in a circle: days follow nights, nights follow days, and each season repeats in a cyclical pattern. Everything in nature exhibits repetitive movements.

Our feeling of time mostly comes from the Earth spinning and going around the sun. Now, think about Earth staying in one spot, not moving closer or farther from the sun. One half is always sunny, and the other is permanently dark. In this situation, how would we know when it is day or night, summer or winter? How would we measure time if we're always facing the sun? Without watches or clocks, would there be time if the Earth doesn't move? It might feel like time has stopped, and we get a glimpse of timelessness. If a part of us lives forever, why are we in such a hurry?

While a linear approach to measuring time, progressing from the past through the present and into the unknown future, has gained significantly in recent centuries, many of the earliest civilizations held a cyclical worldview of time. Throughout history, ancient civilizations depended on cyclical patterns in nature to measure time and synchronize with agricultural and seasonal activities. They observed the sun's movement in the sky to distinguish between days and nights, noted the varying phases of the moon to determine months, and tracked seasonal changes to mark the passage of years.

When we take a moment to slow down and simply observe our lives, we can experience another dimension of timelessness that goes beyond our understanding of time as linear or cyclical. Through awareness and being present in our lives, we may sense a feeling of timelessness and eternity. Our spirit, represented by the *fravashi* within us, doesn't have a starting or ending point. We discover the eternal aspect of ourselves only through our state of being and our connection with the spirit of *fravashi* within us.

By consciously observing our body, thoughts, emotions, words, and deeds, we can detach ourselves from them. Awareness allows us to recognize our immortality when we are not overly attached to external aspects that no longer define us. Conscious dying occurs when we have experienced the immortal part of ourselves, connected to eternity rather than bound by time. While our material existence has a definite beginning and end, there is no birth or death in our core being, our essence, and the spirit of *fravashi*.

In Zarathustra's perspective, we exist in both the corporeal life (visible) and the spiritual world (invisible) simultaneously. In the visible realm, we are bound by linear and cyclical time that are measurable, precise, and concrete, with defined durations. However, in the spiritual world, time is immeasurable, without a calculable beginning or end. On a spiritual level, a part of us transcends time, embracing timelessness and eternity.

If time is measured linearly in a straight line, and cyclical time is represented by a circular pattern, eternity transcends both concepts. It is described as a spiral, originating from unknown and leading to unknowable. Despite the cyclical nature of many phenomena in our physical existence, with births and deaths occurring in repetitive cycles, the awakened spirit within us exists outside the constraints of time, being timeless in a spiral structure.

Zarathustra's perspective portrays life as a progression, where *Vohuman*, the Progressive Spirit, illuminates the Supreme Being (Ahura Mazda), guiding the cosmos towards growth, wisdom, perfection, and goodness. The concept acknowledges the inherent dynamism and advancement in the universe. Unlike the cyclical patterns observed in phenomena like winter and summer, day and night, or sunrise and sunset, life's progression doesn't mean a return to the original state. Although Zarathustra's concept of *Frashokereti* suggests that we will eventually return to our original goodness and paradise will be re-experienced again on Earth, we are not returning exactly to our original state since humans have evolved throughout their existence on Earth. We are not the same as we once were.

While cyclical events repeat, the essence of each occurrence isn't static. Similarly, as seasons come and go, we undergo changes and progress in our lives. The idea in Zarathustra's teaching is that stagnation and dullness align with *Ahriman*, the Wicked Mind, suggesting that true growth and evolution are essential for spiritual well-being. Thus, eternity is perceived as a spiral rather than a perfect circle, signifying the apparent repetition yet continuous progression and growth in life's journey.

We can't feel eternity if we are attached to the mind and stuck on our personality. Eternity is felt when the mind is quiet, and not a single thought hides the sun of consciousness, just like clouds on a starry night. We can only sense our eternal essence when we detach from our personality and the mind. Our understanding of time as a linear progression is very subjective. Time mainly functions as a psychological creation, helping us navigate the constant change of the world around us. Because our minds struggle with uncertainty and need structure, we have developed the concept of time to provide a framework for organizing our experiences into the past, present, and future. Time serves as a tool to reflect on our past, understand our present actions, and anticipate future events.

However, it is important to recognize that this concept of time is unique to human perception and isn't necessarily applicable to the rest of the universe. In reality, time as we perceive it doesn't hold the same significance beyond our own understanding. It exists as a creation of our minds, allowing us to make sense of our existence within the limitation of our consciousness. If we focus our existence in a linear framework only, the cyclical and eternal part of our existence are forgotten and neglected.

We often perceive time as a river flowing beside us. It is easy to think that we are standing still while time rushes past like the water in a river. It is similar to sitting on a train: from inside, it seems like the train isn't moving, but the scenery outside is passing by. Likewise, some suggest that time itself might not be moving; it is our perception that makes it seem that way. The changes we observe aren't time passing; they are changes happening to us. We are the ones who are changing, not time itself. Have you ever seen time? Have you noticed where it starts or ends? When our minds quiet down, and we are fully immersed in the present moment, does time still seem real, or is it just something our minds create? Since we often don't notice our own internal changes, we might mistake them for the passage of time.

When the mind becomes still, we start to see the truth about time. We begin to understand that time doesn't move; it always stays the same. This understanding dawns on us: there is only one unchanging time: the present moment. Time is synonymous with the present, the here and now. We have never lived in the past or the future; we are always living in the present moment. From the day we are born to the day the body dies, we always live "now." We exist in the present throughout our lives, and this "now" stretches across our entire lifespan. Even though we may think about tomorrow or the past, we are never anywhere except now. And wherever we go, space will always become here. Being fully present and conscious in the moment gives us a glimpse of eternity.

The concept of parallel reality suggests that when we transcend linear and cyclical time frames, we can perceive multiple realities simultaneously. In these parallel realities, various events, individuals, and outcomes coexist, especially when the mind and time are no longer constraining factors. Parallel realities occur when different timelines overlap, allowing us to inhabit multiple periods simultaneously. For instance, we might find ourselves existing in both the twenty-first century and another century concurrently or experiencing life as both a caveman and a modern individual at the same time.

A great example is given in the Gospel when Yeshua was asked whether he knew Abraham, who lived thousands of years before him. He answered:

> "Very truly I tell you," Jesus answered,
> "before Abraham was born, I am!"[24]

In this verse, Yeshua is describing his state of "am-ness." Abraham was born and died, but Yeshua still exists in the vertical

---

24 John 8:58 NIV

dimension in his eternal part. He uses the present tense for himself but the past tense for Abraham: "Abraham *was*, I *am*." Abraham's body came and went, but Yeshua's spirit existed before him, exists in his current body, and will continue to exist in eternity. In the parallel reality, he existed two thousand years ago, and he existed one thousand years before his birth with Abraham and before him at the same time.

Jimmy was four years old and wanted to show he was grown up by putting on his shoes. After some struggles, he rushed to his mother to share his success. His mother looked at him and said, "Great job, Jimmy, but you put your shoes on the wrong feet." Jimmy became upset and said, "Mom, trust me, these are not anyone else's feet. They are not wrong. They are mine." Perhaps cyclical and eternal times are not our wrong feet. They still belong to us even if they seem wrong. Maybe, we walk with three feet on Earth and they are all right: linear, cyclical, and eternal feet.

When we are immersed in the present moment, we experience something beyond time: eternity. We start to understand that while we live in mortal bodies, minds, emotions, and events, the essence of our being reflects our eternal nature within the limitations of time. Our consciousness is connected to a higher realm, belonging to the Sublime Consciousness, which radiates from Ahura Mazda. While time is a creation of the mind, consciousness belongs to eternity, to the Supreme Consciousness and Wisdom, to the Eternal Being: Ahura Mazda, thus spake Zarathustra.

MAY THE SPIRIT OF LOVE

AND WISDOM OF MAZDA

BE ALWAYS YOUR GUIDE

www.zarathustra.ca

www.ingramcontent.com/pod-product-compliance
Lightning Source LLC
Chambersburg PA
CBHW050447010526
44118CB00013B/1724